The Home Taxidermist's Handbook

get STUFFED

The Home Taxidermist's Handbook

CHUCK IGLESIAS

Ivy Press

First published in the UK in 2007 by
Ivy Press
210 High Street, Lewes
East Sussex, BN7 2NS, UK.
www.ivy-group.co.uk

Reprinted in 2009

ISBN 13: 978-1-905695-26-3

Printed in China
1 2 3 4 5 6 7 8 9 10

Ivy Press
This book was conceived, designed, and produced by iBall, an imprint of Ivy Press

Creative Director Peter Bridgewater
Publisher Jason Hook
Editorial Director Caroline Earle
Senior Project Editor Rebecca Saraceno
Art Director Kevin Knight
Project Designer Joanna Clinch
Designer Tonwen Jones
Illustrations Josh Halloran

The publishers would like to thank the following for their kind permission to reproduce images featured in this book: Corbis / Yann Arthus-Bertrand 2, 40; Jan Butchofsky-House 25; DK Limited 3, 31; Ute Kaiser / zefa 35; Pawan Kumar 55; Papilio 27; Getty Images / Dorling Kindersley 17, 53; Stone 43.

Cover image of parrot: Getty Images/Dorling Kindersley.

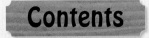

Contents

Taxidermy involves taking the skin off an animal, treating it so that it doesn't rot, and then fixing it over a mold so as to re-create the original shape of the animal. Usually taxidermists attempt to present the animal in some kind of realistic posture, so that if you came across it unaware you might almost think it was alive. We take the view, however, that once the animal is dead, it's dead, and no amount of glass eyes, molded eyelids, and snarling mouthparts is going to convince anyone otherwise. This is particularly the case if the animal in question used to be a faithful family pet.

If you were used to stroking your cat, having your dog fetch the newspaper, or enjoying the various items of dead wildlife that your ferret brought in for you, then it's not going to be much consolation just to have

it stuffed so that it can glare mournfully at you from the corner of the room. But think how much better you would feel if your pet continued to be an active member of your family by fulfilling some useful posthumous role around the house!

This book offers a wealth of projects to help you keep your departed pet in your life. From dachshunds to koi carp, from parrots to gerbils, all animal lovers will find something here to help them cope when that sad day comes.

Use your developing taxidermy skills to make beautiful gifts for your friends. What newly married couple wouldn't appreciate an attractive set of mouse bottle stoppers? The only limit is your imagination.

Taxidermy basics

There are three basic stages in creating a stuffed animal: Skinning, preserving, and mounting. The next pages take you through these basics. Remember that the more you practice, the easier it will become.

Skinning

To skin an animal you will need a sharp knife, some fine scissors, some strong clippers or secateurs, and a lot of newspaper to catch the mess. (If you skin an animal carefully there should be very little blood spillage, but it's sensible to spread out some newspaper anyway.)

The first cut is made straight along the length of the animal, either down the spine or down the belly, depending on how it is to be displayed. The easier method is to slice down the sternum. Lie the animal on its back and make a single incision from the throat to the hind legs. Make sure you use a very sharp blade. Don't press too hard or you will puncture the organs and it will get messy.

Once you have made this incision, simply peel the skin away from the body. It should come away quite easily, but use the scissors to snip any stubborn membranes. When you get to the back legs, slice the skin down toward the foot, and then snip off the foot with the clippers so that the whole foot is attached to the skin. Repeat

this with the other legs. The tailbone of a small mammal can usually be stripped out with a pair of pliers, but for larger mammals you may have to slice the skin down the length of the tail to get the bone out.

Peel the skin up over the head as if you were taking off a sock. When you get to the ears, snip them off with the scissors. Cut around the eyes, taking great care not to damage the eyelids. Then carry on peeling until you get to the nose, which can be snipped off. Now you should have a complete skin with feet, ears, and nose attached.

Preserving

Once the skin is off, you need to treat it so that it doesn't rot. Scrape off any large pieces of flesh adhering to the hide and rub it liberally with borax. Turn the ears, nostrils, eyelids, and tail inside out and make sure you get the borax into every nook and cranny.

Fix the hide to a board flesh side up, with pins, and leave it to dry for a couple of days. If it is a large skin, fold it flesh to flesh and fix it on an inclined surface, with a drip pan underneath to catch the liquid that leaks out. After a couple of days, shake off the excess borax, scrape off any remaining pieces of flesh carefully, and reapply another layer of salt before stretching the skin out flat to dry completely.

Depending on the size of the animal, the hide may become stiff after several days of drying. If it becomes too stiff to work, relax the hide in a solution of brine (lightly salted water) or a proprietary relaxant from a taxidermy supplier. Once it has relaxed, hang it up to dry, but not for so long that it becomes stiff again.

This is sufficient to preserve a hide for mounting. Tanning is a highly specialized and complicated process designed to preserve a hide in a supple condition for making rugs or garments, and isn't necessary for any of the projects in this book.

Mounting

Mounting involves creating a model to give the original animal's shape back to the skin, finishing the stuffed hide with such items as eyes, and placing it on a base or stand of some kind. Taxidermy suppliers offer a range of polyurethane armatures for standard animals, and you can even have these made to order if you supply the measurements of your pet. These armatures are easy to use, though you may need to pad them out with absorbent cotton or papier-maché to get a snug fit.

You can make your own armatures from scratch, which obviously gives you a lot more flexibility. Styrofoam, the type of material used for floral displays, can be easily sculpted with a craft knife to any shape you require. Chicken wire covered in

papier-maché can form the basis for a large armature. Fine wood shavings or excelsior can also be used to stuff a hide that will retain its shape, such as a snakeskin, or balled up with twine to create simple forms for small birds. Absorbent cotton or wadding can be used to pack a hide for a snug fit.

Finishing means just that, the final touches. Eyes and other soft parts obviously cannot be preserved, and a range of different sizes of false eyes are available. Mouthparts and nostrils can be molded from modeling clay, and stiff wire is used to secure wings and tails. Fish scales and birds' beaks and legs will need to be painted or varnished, and all these touches will add quality to your work. They will be a testament to your continued affection for your pet.

Our first project is a bit of a cheat, since it involves a form of taxidermy known as replication. However, there is more than one way to skin a cat, and this is a perfectly acceptable method of modeling an animal, with the added advantage that you can get used to the idea of dealing with dead animals without having to get your hands dirty. The results are entirely original decorations that can't fail to bring cheer to your home.

You will need: one goldfish / shallow tray / fine sand / block of wood / modeling plaster / casting resin / muslin / thin wire / glue / sandpaper / paint

1 Put a layer of sand in the tray and lie your goldfish on its side in the sand. Add more sand until the fish is half-buried. You may need to spread the fins and the tail to get the natural shape. Level out the sand all around the fish with a block of wood.

2 Mix up the modeling plaster so that it is the consistency of pancake batter and pour it over the fish. Let it set hard, and then pour over another layer for extra strength.

3 When the plaster has set, turn the fish out of the mold. You should now have an impression of one side of

your fish. Repeat the process for the other side so that you have two molds.

4 Fill the molds with casting resin, first putting small pieces of muslin cut to shape on the tail and fins to give extra strength to the cast. Put a piece of wire bent into a U shape into the mouth or near the dorsal fin of one of the halves to make a hanger.

5 When the resin casts are completely dry, take them out of the molds, glue the two halves of your fish together (you may need to sandpaper any rough edges to get a good fit) and then paint your fish. You can re-use the molds to make a shoal of pet replicas to enliven your festive display.

he great thing about hamsters is that they don't last long. Although pet shops and websites will tell you that their average lifespan is about two years, most owners find that they die with fairly monotonous regularity after about six months, so it doesn't take long to get a decent stock of them. You can use just one hamster, but you get a better display if you have more, and for dinner parties it's ideal to have one for each place setting.

You will need: four hamsters / four small mammal armatures / pipe cleaners / modeling adhesive / four wooden mounts / four tea lights

1 Skin the hamsters and dry the skins as described on pages 8–11 (cut down the spine rather than the belly). Take each armature and use a craft knife or scalpel to cut off the forelegs (these armatures are usually made of polyurethane so they are quite easy to cut). Take the pipe cleaners and make new forelegs (use the ones you have just cut off for size), fixing these firmly to the torso with modeling adhesive.

Your dinner guests will adore these little helpers!

2 To get the skin onto the armature, it's best to put the arms in first, a bit like putting on a surgical gown. Once the skin is in place, fix the hamster to its stand. Make sure that the hamster is mounted firmly on the stand so that it doesn't tip forward when it is holding the tea light. Then simply bend the arms round slightly and place the tea light in the hamster's grip. (Set its arms away from its face or its nose could go up in flames.)

The most difficult processes with birds are skinning and mounting them so that they look lifelike. This bird project is one of the first in this book because it does not require any mounting and so gives you a chance to practice one of the difficult techniques without worrying about the other. If you don't have a canary, a parakeet will work just as well.

You will need: one canary / light cord / wood shavings / twine / heavy grade wire / absorbent cotton / fine wire / two eyes / varnish

1 Make an incision down the breastbone from the neck and peel the skin away from the flesh. When you get to the legs, peel the skin down to the leg joint and sever the leg at the joint. Cut off the tail but be careful not to cut through the roots of the tail feathers or they will fall out.

2 Moving up to the wings, cut them off where they are fixed to the canary's shoulders, and then peel the skin over the head as if you were removing a balaclava. Don't cut through the beak.

3 Now you should have a canary suit with the wings and lower legs

attached, and the skull attached at the beak. You will need to clean all the flesh off the skull and the wing bones, and drill a small hole in the top of the skull for the light cord.

4 Make a body shape with the wood shavings and twine and push a length of sharpened heavy-gauge wire through from top to bottom, bending it up at the bottom to secure it. Ease this armature into the skin, pushing the wire through the hole in the skull and pad out any loose areas with absorbent cotton. Fold the wings to the sides of the bird and tie them in place with fine wire (the feathers will hide this). Add the eyes and varnish the beak before attaching the light cord to the wire protruding from the bird's skull.

hese miniature turtles are charming pets, as long as you keep your fingers away from their beaks, and this project carries their charm into the hereafter. You may have guessed that this is another replication project. Put the terrapin in the freezer for a couple of hours before you begin so that its legs remain in position when you cast it.

You will need: one terrapin / deep tray / sand / wood block / modeling plaster / casting resin / spherical jingly bells / string wire / some lengths of dowel

1 Put a layer of sand in the tray deep enough to accommodate the terrapin lying on its side, add more sand until it is half-covered, and level out with a wood block as before.

2 Pour the plaster mix over, and try to ensure that it runs into the gaps under the shell at the head and the tail.

3 Repeat the process for the other side (you may need to pop the terrapin back in the freezer between sides) so that you have two molds. This time you want a hollow cast, so instead of filling the mold with resin, pour enough in to cover the mold to a depth of a quarter inch or so (the legs will fill up but that's okay). Spread it with a stiff brush if necessary.

A lovely finishing touch for a child's playroom.

4 Finish the casts as you did for the fish (see *page 13*), but before glueing the sides together, put a few bells inside. Make a small hole in the beak and hang your terrapin where it will catch the breeze. You can use the mold to make more terrapins and tie them to a crossframe for a more musical effect.

This is an extremely easy starter project, and would be suitable for introducing a child to the art of taxidermy. If you do not have a chinchilla, you can use a gerbil or hamster instead.

You will need: one chinchilla (or a gerbil or hamster or guinea pig) / excelsior and twine, or styrofoam / strong wire / ear liners / modeling clay / a house brick / green felt / cotton wadding / fake grass or crepe paper / papier–maché

1 Skin the chinchilla (you should use a ventral abdominal incision) and preserve the hide as normal. Make the mannikin from excelsior and twine or carved styrofoam. The chinchilla is a relatively straightforward body shape, although you will need to use ear liners to support its big ears.

2 Model the legs with modeling clay, leaving about two feet of wire protruding from the feet.

3 Fix the hide back on to the model. When it has dried, wrap the leg wires around the brick to secure it. Cut a panel of styrofoam the same

size as the bottom of the brick and tape it securely onto the underside.

4 Cover the brick with green felt lined with cotton wadding. It's easiest to cut a single piece to run around all four sides and then sew another panel onto the bottom of this strip to create a pouch into which the brick will fit. You will need to cut the felt for the top of the brick to fit around the chinchilla, but you can cover up the joins by glueing on imitation grass made from crepe paper or bought from a model shop.

You can bring a personal touch to this traditional family game by having an ex-family member take part. You could also use the rabbit's ears as a rack for your jewelry.

You will need: one rabbit (long-eared) / balsa wood / modeling clay / bag of sand / drill / copper pipe / cotton wadding / wooden base

1 The main challenge with this project is making sure that the rabbit stays upright to catch the horseshoes. Once you have skinned the animal and prepared the hide you will need to create the armature. Sculpt the head and torso from a piece of balsa wood to create an upright mannikin. The feet and legs can be made from modeling clay, which allows for more precision.

2 When the armature is complete, scoop a hollow out of the rump end big enough to accommodate a bag of sand, which will act as ballast. At the top end, drill two holes down from the head where the ears will sit, into which you can slide two equal lengths of copper pipe. These should protrude from the top of the head to the length of the ears and be

anchored well inside the torso for
stability. Fill out the ear shapes with
papier-mâché or cotton wadding.

3 Fit the hide over the mannikin,
starting with the ears at the top,
and insert a bag of sand into the rump
before sewing up the incision. Mount
the model on a solid wooden base. If
you don't like the idea of throwing
things at your rabbit use it as a rack
for your horseshoes instead.

f you don't have a hat, this exotic addition to your hallway will make you
go out and get one. You could also hang a scarf or umbrella on it, as long
as it's not too heavy.

You will need: one iguana / excelsior and twine or styrofoam / modeling clay /
stout wire / papier-maché / tree branch / back plate

1 When you skin the iguana you
should stop at the head, just
behind the ears. The skin is tightly
fixed to the head and it's easier to
preserve the reptile with its skull
intact. You will need to remove the
brains, the eyes, and other soft parts,
and completely clean out the skull
cavity with plenty of borax. You should
also skin the body out to the tip of the
tail, cutting on the side that is going to
be facing the wall.

2 The main body shape can be
built up using the excelsior and
twine method. The feet and legs are
best modeled out of clay, as are the
soft tissues of the head. When it comes
to the tail, take some stout wire and
bend it to a long hook shape, then
flesh this out with papier-maché. The
tail should be turned up at the end to
hold the hat. Push the protruding end
of the wire through the main body
form, bending it over to secure it.

3 Fit the skin onto the mannikin and sew up the incision. For the stand, it's a good idea to use an actual tree branch, which will look more natural than a wooden base. You can fix the branch to a back plate, which can be attached to the wall. The iguana should be mounted such that its tail hangs down from the branch so that you can put your hat on it.

Tortoises are hard to preserve in their entirety using conventional methods. The easiest way to preserve them whole, as with most reptiles, is to freeze-dry them, which will set you back several hundred dollars. This project allows you to keep a memento of your pet without the expense. If you want to use the clock in the bedroom, paint the clock hands and numbers with luminous paint so you can read them in the dark.

You will need: one tortoise / some clear varnish or lacquer / drill / clock mechanism / wire

1 Turn the tortoise upside down and cut along the underside of the carapace where it joins the lower part of the shell. Now slide a sharp blade between the skin of the tortoise and the shell until the body of the animal comes away. Cover the inside of the shell with borax and put in the fridge for a day so that the flesh softens.

2 With a tablespoon, scrape all the flesh out from inside the shell and break up the bony structure where the spinal cord was at the dome of the shell. You need to be sure that you get all the flesh out of the shell otherwise it will smell.

3 Wash out the shell with lots of water, apply another coating of borax, and leave it for several days to dry out completely. Seal the inside and outside with some clear varnish.

4 Drill a hole in the shell for the spindle of the clock hands and mount the clock mechanism inside the shell (you can get one from a specialty store or else just take one from a standard kitchen clock). Reattach the clock hands and paint numbers on the shell with enamel paint, or simply leave it plain. To hang the clock, fix a wire loop to the top of the shell.

Dog TV remote holder

One problem with modern life is the peripatetic nature of the various remote control devices that we need to keep our technology at our fingertips. No sooner do you put the machine down than it mysteriously migrates to some other part of the house (particularly if there are children around). This project supplies the solution, and permits your faithful family servant to continue in service long after his or her demise.

You will need: one dog (mid-size such as border collie or retriever is best) / dog armature / modeling clay / heavy-grade wire

1 The main challenge with this project is the reconstruction of the lower jaw. There are a number of ways to address this. One is to manufacture a lower jaw using heavy-grade wire mesh and modeling clay, and attach this to the dog armature, keeping the jaws slightly open.

2 A more satisfactory method is to retain the skull after you have skinned the animal and discarded the brain and other perishable elements. This needs to be thoroughly cleaned and dried out, and then you can replace the head of the armature with the actual skull.

3 You will need to fix the lower jaw, which of course no longer has the necessary tendons and muscles to keep it in place, either by glueing it or wiring it into position. A process of trial and error will allow you to gauge the correct aperture. Once this is complete, simply pop the remote into the dog's mouth, and you will never lose it again.

The most loyal television remote holder in the world!

These **charming** cruets make an extremely attractive accompaniment to the hamster tea light holders, although you won't want to confine their use to special occasions. Gerbils are sociable animals and so you should keep them as pairs, making them ideal for this project. The tricky part is the armature, since you will have to sculpt it yourself in order to accommodate the jars.

You will need: two gerbils / styrofoam or balsa wood / two narrow screwtop jars / wooden bases

1 First skin the gerbils and preserve the hides. You will need to make a hole in the skin on the crown of the head, but this is best left until later.

2 Carve the armature from styrofoam or balsa wood to create an upright model. You will then need to scoop out a cavity to hold the glass jars. These should fit snugly so that they don't fall out when the cruets are shaken. Don't cut right through the bottom of the armature.

3 Slide the skin on to the armature, sew it up, and then make a small incision in the crown above the opening in the armature. Slice away

from the center toward the sides of the opening, and glue the flaps of skin firmly down on the inside.

4 Fix the gerbils onto round or square wooden bases, a little wider than the bottom of the model, and slip the glass jars inside. These should fit snugly and not protrude too far from the top of each gerbil's head.

Large dog burglar deterrent

This project is more a matter of wiring and theatrical placement than taxidermy as such. There's no reason why your Doberman or German Shepherd should not continue to perform as a house guard even when its burglar-chasing days are long gone. Other than its size, there's no difference between the preparation of this model and the dog on pages 28–29, though there is no need to retain the skull this time.

You will need: one large dog / movement sensors / light source / recording of your dog barking and CD or MP3 player / baby rocker (optional)

1 You will need to fix a PIR movement sensor on the outside of your house overlooking the driveway. This should be wired up to a CD or MP3 player, which will replay the recording of your dog's bark. Borrow a scary dog from a friend to make the recording if necessary.

2 Wire up a low level light source to the PIR sensor. Place the dog in an upstairs window overlooking the driveway, so the light will throw its outline onto the window. From ground level an intruder will see only a menacing silhouette and won't be able to tell that the dog is no real threat.

3 For added sophistication, mount the dog on one of those moving trolleys that are used to rock babies to sleep in their buggies. This should also be wired to the PIR switch, so that unwelcome guests are greeted by a volley of barks and the dimly lit moving outline of a large hound.

He is your friend, your partner, your defender, your dog.

Cat foot-warmer

Few things are more comforting than a faithful friend cuddling up to you and keeping you warm. If you don't want to give up this cozy relationship after your cat has died, try this project. Use your beloved foot-warmer while watching TV, or leave it curled at the end of your bed.

You will need: one cat (long-haired varieties are particularly good) / excelsior and twine or styrofoam / zipper / heat-retaining gel pack

1 Skin the cat using a ventral incision and preserve the hide. Make the mannikin using excelsior and twine or styrofoam so that the cat is lying on its side curled around. Arch the cat's body slightly on the side where your feet go so that you will be able to tuck them in. You then need to create a hollow in the mannikin to accommodate the gel pack.

2 Sew up the hide and insert a zipper over the hollow in the mannikin. When styling the head, you will want to make your cat look asleep as it would have been when it was actually warming your feet. This will give you good practice in modeling eyelids from clay, which is one of the great art forms of taxidermy.

3 When the model has dried out completely, simply pop the gel pack into the hollow, zip it shut, and use it to warm your feet.

Siamese cat bedside lamp

This project enables you to preserve your beloved Siamese as a guardian spirit, like the Egyptian cat goddess Bast, to watch over you while you sleep. You can use other breeds of cat, too—Burmese cats work particularly well, as do other Asian breeds.

You will need: one Siamese cat / glue or wire / cat armature / zipper / table lamp kit, or the component parts

1 Skin the cat in the usual way, making the first incision down the spine, but retain the skull. Clean all the flesh from the bone and extract the brain, then treat the skull with preservative and let it dry out thoroughly. Glue or wire the jaws shut.

2 Sculpt or buy an armature that shows the cat sitting upright. Remove the head and fix the light socket to the neck. You will probably need to screw the socket to a wooden base plate and then glue this onto the armature. The light bulb should not protrude too far into the skull. You should also make a hole right down through the armature in order to accommodate the electric cable.

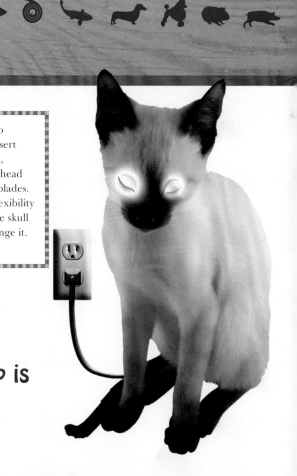

3 Before you fix the hide onto the armature you should insert a zipper into the dorsal incision, running from the crown of the head down to between the shoulder blades. This should give you enough flexibility to be able to slip the hide off the skull and access the light bulb to change it.

This lovely lamp is the cat's meow!

Parrots are a good size for this project, and their plumage will brighten up your study. If you don't have a pair of parrots you can make just one bookend and use it at the end of a fixed shelf.

You will need: a pair of parrots / stiff wire / material for armatures / lumber for stand / length of dowel or tree branch

1 Skin the birds as described in the canary project earlier (see *pages 16–17*), remembering to take care with the tail feathers. Make an armature with excelsior and twine to fit the body of each bird.

2 Because these birds will be standing up you will also need to support the legs and the tail. Make a small hole in the foot of each bird and push the sharpened end of a piece of wire up through the hole and along the leg bone under the bird's skin, taking care not to puncture the skin. Estimate where the legs should join the body and push the wire straight through the armature and out the other side, bending it back to secure it. Bend the leg slightly to prevent it from sliding down the wire, and leave a couple of inches of wire protruding from the foot.

3 Put the skin onto the armature and sew it up, folding and binding the wings to the body with thin wire. Make a U-shape from a piece of wire and push the ends into the model under the tail, leaving the bent end sticking out to support the feathers.

4 For the base you will need to make two wooden L-shapes. Choose an attractively veneered wood. You will also need a perch for the birds, either made from dowel or a tree branch of the right size. Drill holes though the perch for the foot wires and pass these though the holes, wrapping the wires around to secure them.

Poodle coffee table

A poodle is a handsome creature, and this project will produce a beautiful centerpiece for any living room and an appropriate tribute to your elegant companion. You can trim your poodle's coat in a variety of ways too, to create a dazzling display of canine indoor topiary. Use a dog shampoo to remove any coffee spills.

You will need: one standard poodle / medium-size dog armature / sheet of glass / two leather straps or stainless-steel bands

1 The first thing you will need to do is take careful measurements from your pet. You should establish its girth just behind the shoulders and just in front of the hind legs. You should also measure its collar size at the base of its neck and its length from neck to rump.

2 You will need to commission a glazier to supply a rectangular piece of shatterproof glass that will sit on the dog's back, with a cutout to go around the neck. This should have two holes drilled in it at the points on the dog's torso where you measured its girth.

3 The dog is skinned and the hide preserved in the usual way. The armature, however, needs some special preparation. Two wooden strips need to be inserted transversely into the armature at the points on the dog's torso where you measured its girth. These will act as anchorage points for the harness. The modified armature can be inserted into the hide and the model completed in the usual way.

4 For the harness you will need two stout leather straps, which are fixed with rivets onto the glass table top (stainless-steel bands can be used for a more contemporary look). The glass top can then be placed squarely on to the dog's back, and the leather bands pulled tight and screwed securely into the wooden strips on either side.

Mouse bottle stopper

Completing your rodent-themed dinner service, this simple bottle stopper means that you need never drink alone. You can use these attractive stoppers for all your oils, vinegars, and wines.

You will need: one mouse / excelsior and twine or styrofoam / strong wire / bottle stopper

1 You will need a bottle stopper with a wooden handle to which you will be able to fix the stuffed mouse (you can often get beautifully carved wooden stoppers from craft shops).

2 Skin the animal and preserve the hide as usual. Given the animal's size you may want to preserve the mouse's skull so as not to have to remodel it.

3 Make the mannikin from excelsior and twine or styrofoam. You should take account of the shape of the wine stopper you are using when modeling the body, so that you create a realistic shape that will look as though the mouse is climbing up the handle. Fix the skin onto the mount, leaving enough wire protruding from the feet to fix the animal to the stopper, and put it aside to dry.

This vintage mouse pulls out the stops!

4 Put the model up next to the handle of the stopper and mark where you will need to drill holes to take the wires from the feet. It is a good idea also to carve a groove into the handle where the wire will wrap around it so that it will lie flush. Fix the model to the handle, hiding the ends of the wires under its body.

5 When you take the stopper out of a bottle, be sure to grip the handle as well as the mouse so as not to damage the model.

Dachshund baby cushion

The obvious thing to do with a dachshund, given its distinctive shape, is to make a draft stopper. But leaving a faithful retainer to lie in the cold for years on end would be the height of ingratitude, so this project is designed to bring your pet back into the bosom of its family.

You will need: one dachshund / excelsior and twine / ear liners / no-slip rubber (optional)

1 Skin the animal and preserve the hide as explained on pages 9–10. This model needs to be comfortable to the touch, so it is better to make an armature with excelsior and twine, rather than using a polyurethane mannikin. The dog's body is quite easy to stuff, and you can use clay for the legs and head.

2 You should pose the dog in a shallow V-shape to make a support for the child, with the legs tucked up out of the way. You will need to skin the ears and insert flexible ear liners. Short ears stand up naturally when you sew a hide tightly onto an armature, but longer ears need some support if they are to look realistic.

3 You may want to fix some non-slip rubber onto the bottom of the model so that it does not slide on smooth floors when your baby is leaning on it. The curved shape helps to prop the baby up safely, and the ears offer opportunities for play to develop motor skills.

Koi carp tie rack

This is a handy way of keeping your ties in good order while giving a new lease of life to a prized specimen. It is also more straightforward than most fish projects because the only sections that you need to preserve are the head and the tail.

You will need: one koi carp / fish head mold / fiberglass resin sheet / paint / clear varnish / heavy-grade wire / epoxy resin / piano wire / brass hook

1 Take the fish and fillet it, taking care not to damage the spine or ribs. Cut off the tail and head. Skin the head and dry all three elements in the usual way. Fix the skin of the head onto the mold following the manufacturer's instructions and mount the tail using a fiberglass resin sheet. The scales will of course become dull, and you will want to reproduce the original coloring with some good quality metallic paint, or with an airbrush and a coating of clear varnish.

2 Now you need to reassemble the three elements of the fish, using the heavy-grade wire as an extra spinal column for strength. This can be screwed into the head mold at one end and bound to the spine with piano wire. The tail, which

An impressive rack for any closet!

does not have to be load-bearing, can simply be attached with some epoxy resin. Fix the brass hook into the nose of the fish so that it can be hung on the rail in your closet. Then simply drape your ties over the horizontal ribs.

A striking addition to any library or study, this attractive display stand can be adapted to make a photo frame or magazine prop. It would also make an ideal bookstand in any cook's kitchen.

You will need: three rats / small mammal armatures / strong wire / pipe cleaners / lumber for frame

1 This project calls for some carpentry skills and a bit of imagination in creating the armatures. First skin and preserve the rats in the usual way. Then build the book frame. This should be made from narrow strips of timber to produce a rectangular frame the size of an open book.

2 Two of the rats will be standing upright to support the frame. These call for relatively straightforward armatures, though you will need to use strong wire for the legs. The third rat will be leaning over the top of the frame to hold the book open with its front legs. These legs should be constructed from pipe cleaners or flexible wire as they will need to bend.

3 Fix the two upright rats at points to support the ends of the frame with their front legs. You can leave their wired back legs freestanding or fix them to an optional wooden base. Attach the third rat to the top of the frame (you will need to drill holes in it to take the wires from its back legs). Place your book on the frame and bend the top rat's arms down to hold it open.

Insect jewelry

You can make unusual and distinctive jewelry for him and her with these insect projects. Each one is a unique gift with a personal touch. You could also use them to adorn cushion covers or napkin rings.

You will need: cockroaches, stag beetles, stick insects / jewelry mounts / casting resin / clear lacquer or varnish

1 Insects are fascinating pets and require very little care. Even cockroaches have an enormous fan club in spite of their reputation as pests. Preserving insects is quite straightforward, since their hard exoskeleton enables you to preserve their shape without shrinkage. As they dry out, the soft parts shrivel, leaving the external features intact.

2 You should suit the type of jewelry to the insect at hand. For instance, a three-inch Madagascan hissing cockroach would be an unwieldy ring but an ideal brooch or pendant. Stick insects are suited to tiepins, while sun beetles and frog beetles make beautiful earrings. Different types of jewelry mounts are available from craft shops.

3 It is a good idea to set the insect on a cushion of clear resin so delicate parts such as legs and antennae are not damaged. When this has set hard, paint the insect with clear lacquer to protect it and bring out the natural colors. Then simply glue the insect and its resin pillow onto the mount.

51

Parrot key rack

This striking and colorful keyrack will be a practical and beautiful addition to your hall or kitchen. If you have a lot of keys to store you may obtain better results with a larger pet bird, calculating the wingspan carefully to allow for the correct number of attachments.

You will need: one parrot / materials for armature / strong wire / wood for the stand

1 The procedure for skinning the bird is the same as that for the other bird projects. The great thing about preserving birds is that the skin cures on the model, so all you need to do is make sure that all the flesh is taken off the skin and bones, and sprinkle everything with borax before moving on to the next step.

2 As with the bookends, this is a freestanding model so you will need to wire the legs and tail. However, the wings will also have to be supported, because these are displayed open rather than folded back to the bird's body. The procedure is the same as for the legs. Beginning at the end that was severed from the body, push the wire along the wingbone under the skin

until it reaches the tip, leaving several inches of wire protruding at the shoulder. Wrap the wire once around the end of the wingbone and then push the end right through the body armature and bend it back around to secure it.

3 To make the key hooks, push short lengths of wire (three for each wing) through the wing close to the bone and wrap them around the wire to secure them.

4 Make splints for the wings from strips of stiff card pinned together, one on each side of the wing, to prevent the feathers from curling while the model dries. You can make a perch for the parrot to stand on a table, or fix one directly to the wall.

Python laundry basket

Reptiles such as snakes are ideal candidates for freeze-drying, because their moisture content is relatively low. You can use the freeze-drying method for a medium-sized snake, which can be coiled around to create a pen holder or wastepaper basket. However, for a larger snake, the old-fashioned method shown here is a better approach.

You will need: one python / snakeskin preservative / several pounds of wood shavings / modeling clay to make eyes and mouth / wooden skewers / lining material

1 Lay the python out lengthwise (you may need to find a neighbor with a long hallway) and skin it from head to tail, retaining the skull. Tack the skin onto a board, flesh side out, and paint with (snakeskin) tanning solution. It will take a week or so to dry out.

2 Beginning at the tail, sew the two sides of the skin together to create a tube, fixing a strip of lining material on the inside of the seam so that there are no gaps.

So much classier than wicker!

3 As you sew along the seam, stop every foot or so and fill the tube with wood shavings, packing them down well. Continue until the snake is completely stuffed. Add the eyes and mouthparts modeled from clay.

4 Coil the snake around, fixing the coils in place on top of each other with wooden cooking skewers until the snake is built up into a tall container.

5 Make a bag from an old sheet or lining material and fix it inside the snake coil to hold your laundry.

Though the hedgehog isn't always thought of as a pet, many of our backyards are visited by a friendly example. Encourage it to come again with some canned pet food in a bowl. And if a cold snap sets in, or you happen to live on a busy road, chances are that you will soon have access to a prickly corpse for this project.

You will need: one hedgehog / insecticide / small mammal armature / absorbent cotton or papier-mâché / mounting stand

1 If your starting point is roadkill, you will need to check first that the hide is relatively intact. And whether or not your hedgehog comes lifesize or flat-packed, you will need to wear stout gloves when handling it to avoid the prickly spines.

2 Hedgehogs are notoriously verminous, so you should treat the body with insecticide before you do anything else. When the fleas are all dead, brush off the insecticide and insects and skin the animal in the usual way.

3 The treating and mounting of the animal follows the standard procedure, but in order for the letters to sit neatly on the animal's back you will need to carve a section from the top of the armature to flatten it out. Compensate for the bagginess of the skin by stuffing the sides with absorbent cotton or papier-maché.

4 Fix the animal on all four feet on an optional stand and pop your letters or memoranda between the prickles on its back.

For the collector: garden chess set

If you are the kind of person who collects strays, if you work at an animal shelter, of if you have friends who wish to preserve their lamented pets, you may find yourself with a whole set of animal corpses on your hands. If so, you can create a fun memorial yard game.

You will need: Lots of animals

1 Stoke up the barbecue grill, invite all your taxidermy contacts over, and remember to ask them to bring a stuffed friend. The fun of this project comes from deciding which of the animals that turn up is going to be which piece. The small rodents are good for pawns and there are likely to be more of them than anything else. Castles are solid and slow-moving, so tortoises are perfect.

2 Choose cats for the nimble knights, and maybe rabbits for the bishops. The royal animals (assuming no one shows up with a lion) are best left to a couple of good-size dogs, perhaps retrievers or afghans. You can mark out squares on your lawn with whitewash, or you can create a giant chess board by painting a sheet or tarp. Have fun!

Terminal terminology

armature—this is the body shape onto which you fix the skin. It can be a proprietary model made from polyurethane or something you create yourself from styrofoam, papier-maché, or other materials.

borax—soft white crystals used to clean and disinfect animal skins after they are removed.

ear liners—special supports for use when stuffing an animal with big ears.

excelsior—soft wood shavings used as packing material, which can be balled up and bound with twine to create simple body shapes.

fleshing—removing all the flesh and other perishable material from the hide, very important to prevent the spread of ruinous bacteria.

freeze drying—a method of preserving an animal by freezing it, then reducing the surrounding air pressure to draw out the water content in the form of vapor; this prevents the flesh from rotting.

mannikin—this is an alternative name for an armature.

replication—method of modeling an animal from accurate measurements and photographs, often used by fishermen who don't want to kill whatever they have caught.

styrofoam—a type of polystyrene foam that can be carved and shaped.

tanning—processing a skin to make it soft and supple for use in garment or rug making.

Further reading & useful websites

Home Book of Taxidermy and Tanning
Gerald J. Grantz
Not as comprehensive for the beginner as
Russell Tinsley, but has stood the test of time.

**Practical Taxidermy—A Manual of
Instruction to the Amateur in Collecting,
Preserving, and Setting Up Natural
History Specimens of All Kinds**
Montagu Browne
A nineteenth-century book which nonetheless
has much useful information for the modern
stuffer. Also has charming woodcuts.

The Taxidermy Guide
Russell Tinsley
Now in a third edition, the Bible for anyone
who has a dead animal on their hands and
needs to know what to do with it.

**Amy Ritchie's taxidermy
www.amystaxidermy.com**
Proof that stuffing dead animals is not just
for the boys.

**Taxidermy.net
http://www.taxidermy.net**
More than you could possibly want to know
about the hows and whys of stuffing.

**WASCO taxidermy hobby kits
www.taxidermy.com/cat/01/kits.html**
Basic kits to get you started.

There are also taxidermy magazines such as:
**Breakthrough
www.breakthroughmagazine.com
Taxidermy Today
www.taxidermytoday.com**
These magazines will give you the latest news
from the world of taxidermy and the most
up-to-date methods and materials to achieve
that professional look.

Index

Index & acknowledgments

I would like to thank my wife for all her helpful suggestions; my children for alerting me to the presence of any potentially useful dead animals in our neighborhood; and Mitzi, Scamp, Jessie, Wolf, Sonny and Cher, Bozo, Charlie, Bluey, Richie, Fred, Sandy, Petra, Cheech, Bullseye, Milo, Tallulah, Coco, Zoe, Shadrach, General Gordon, Starsky and Hutch, Socks, Foucault, and Patsy, without whom these projects could not have been completed and to whose memory this book is affectionately dedicated.